EAT FEAR FOR BREAKFAST

BREAK FREE & BOLDY WALK
IN YOUR GOD-GIVEN PURPOSE

Devotional & Journal

Copyright © 2024 FaithInspiration Network

Publishing services provided by DWilson & Associates, LLC.

DW
DWilson & Associates, LLC

All rights reserved. Printed in the United States of America.
No part of this book may be used or reproduced in any manner whatsoever without written permission from the author.

All contributors to this work have duly consented to the use of their personal data, facts, recollections, memories, and/or experiences found herein. They are aware that the end and intended result was mass production and publication in connection with this work. As such, they have agreed without equivocation or caveat to indemnify, defend, and hold harmless the collaborator and publisher of this material, along with their affiliates, officers, directors, employees, and agents from any and all claims, damages, expenses, and liabilities arising out of or in connection with the use of such personal data, facts, recollections, memories, and experiences, including any claims of infringement of intellectual property rights or violation of privacy rights.

ISBN: 9798334266537

This book is presented by

Faith
INSPIRATION NETWORK

The place where FAITH lives out LOUD

We inspire you to embrace a more courageous faith journey in your ministry, business, community and family life through:

EQUIPPING SESSIONS
DAILY ENCOURAGEMENT
COLLABORATIVE PROJECTS
EVENTS

WE INSPIRE YOU
To Activate Your Gifts to Do More for God

WE EMPOWER YOU
To Take the Next Steps

WE EQUIP YOU
To Elevate Your Message and Testimony

WE CONNECT YOU
To Increase Collaboration for Greater Impact

FAITHINSPIRATION NETWORK IS A 501(3)C NONPROFIT

DEDICATION

This book is dedicated to my grandmother, Ellanora Williams; my mother, Ella Chaney Williams Patrick; and my sister, Carolyn Irene Patrick Green — three women who met fear on a daily basis — and walked right past it.

The Lord is my light and my salvation;
whom shall I fear?
The Lord is the stronghold of my life;
of whom shall I be afraid?

Psalm 27:1

INTRODUCTION

By Dorothy P. Wilson

Founder, FaithInspiration Network

This devotional was created for women, by women, to help women break free of the spirit of fear. Twenty-two women of faith will tell you how the Holy Spirit and the word of God has encouraged their faith to overcome. As you read their stories, you'll find yourself, and when you do, take note of how God touched the lives of these women and transformed their thinking. Claim the words he spoke to them for yourself! What he did for them, he will do for you!

You'll come to understand that being fearless doesn't mean you have an absence of fear. No, it means that even when you are afraid and vulnerable, your faith in God, his love for you and his promises for you will empower you to not only stand against fear but also to walk forward with confidence.

This project has a deeply personal meaning for me. As a young girl, I lived in constant fear. I never knew when "the other shoe would drop," meaning when my father, who suffered with the disease of alcoholism, would become even more violent and abusive, sending my mom, me and my siblings running through the woods for our lives. I was already shy, and this fearful environment certainly didn't help with developing my confidence.

As I grew into adult life, I became an overachiever who played all the strategies in my head before moving forward. This was my coping mechanism. I didn't have to be fearful if I had visited all the possible scenarios and had prepared myself to overcome and win at every turn. Does this sound familiar to you?

By the time I reached my 30s, I had a very successful career — but there was one problem. I was now sitting in the boardroom with the CEOs and VPs, and fear too often kept me from speaking up, being assertive. I was now running with the big dogs and had to think on the fly.

MOMENT OF TRANSFORMATION

One day I got tired — no, not just tired, but sick and tired — of being stuck on the wall.

Internally, I was roaring: "NO MORE!"

This Bible verse pierced me, twisted me, pounded me and stood me up:

"The Lord is on my side; I will not fear. What can man do to me?" (Psalm 118:6)

It's amazing how 16 words can change your whole life! With these words shouting in my heart, I took my eyes off of people — horizontal thinking, or person-to-person focus. And I began to think vertically, me-to-God focus.

My new way of thinking: I am who he says I am, and that is what matters. When I can meditate on his teachings and who

EAT FEAR FOR BREAKFAST

God says I am during my morning time with him, I'm able to chew fear up and swallow it as I walk into my day.

It's time for you to eat fear for breakfast, too. It's time for you to roar, "NO MORE!"

The world is filled with successful women who refuse to allow their fear to hold them back. They get up every day and march toward greatness. These women aren't so different from other women. They doubt themselves. They stay up worrying at night about their children, job, businesses, marriage, ministry, money. And yep, they fear they're not doing things right.

Sound like you? Yeah, me, too.

What makes them different is they've decided to stare fear down every day.

They've learned that the very act of confronting and overcoming fears builds strength that keeps building until their foundation is rock solid.

It's time to stop shrinking back. It's time to stop compromising.

It's time to EAT FEAR FOR BREAKFAST.

Dorothy

EAT FEAR FOR BREAKFAST

Today's Scripture

Fear not, for I am with you; be not dismayed, for I am your God; I will strengthen you, I will help you, I will uphold you with my righteous right hand.

Isaiah 41:10

Day 1

FAITH OVER FEAR: TRUSTING GOD'S PROMISES

By Dr. Sanja Rickette Stinson

When I think of "eating fear for breakfast," what comes to mind is this memory: As the founding CEO of a nonprofit organization, I was scheduled to speak at a local community event. The night before, I was filled with anxiety and thoughts of backing out. But I remembered Isaiah 41:10 and chose to meditate on its promises. As I stood before the audience, I felt an overwhelming sense of peace and strength. My words flowed more smoothly than ever before, and I could see the impact they were having on the listeners. It was a powerful reminder that when we step out in faith, God meets us where we are and equips us for His purposes.

I know that many people think of FEAR as an acronym for "False Evidence Appearing Real." But when I think of fear from a biblical perspective, I choose to consider the acronym to be "Faith, Empowerment, Assurance, Resilience."

Fear is a common experience, but it doesn't have to be a paralyzing one. For me, fear was a constant companion because of my severe speech impediment. The thought of speaking in front of others would trigger intense anxiety and self-doubt. I would worry about stumbling over words, being misunderstood, or even ridiculed. My fear was rooted in the false evidence that my speech impediment defined my ability to communicate and connect with others. However, God's Word provided a different perspective, one that empowered me to confront and overcome my fears.

Isaiah 41:10 became a lifeline for me. It reminded me that I am not alone in my struggles and that God's strength is greater than my weaknesses.

Faith is the first step to overcoming fear. Isaiah 41:10 reassures us that God is with us. Instead of fear, I had to rely on faith in the promises of God, faith in God's presence, and faith in God's power. Learning to internalize my faith caused me to pivot my focus from my limitations to God's limitless ability. It led me to trust that God could and would use my voice, despite my impediment, to encourage and inspire others.

Empowerment comes from believing and knowing that God has already equipped me for the tasks I have been called to do. This verse tells us: "I will strengthen you; I will help you." It is a powerful reminder that as kingdom-minded believers, we are not left to face fear on our own. God's strength is made perfect in our weakness (2 Corinthians 12:9). Personally, leaning on God's strength was a guiding light, giving me the courage to speak, knowing that it was God who would empower my words and actions.

Assurance is the confidence we have in God's unfailing support. Isaiah 41:10 promises that God will uphold all who believe and trust him with his righteous right hand. This assurance gave me the confidence to step out in faith. I realized that my fear of speaking was based on the false evidence of my perceived inadequacies. God's assurance, however, was rooted in his perfect ability to sustain and support me.

Resilience is the ability to bounce back from setbacks and continue moving forward. It's about facing challenges head-on and trusting that God is working all things for our good. My journey with my speech impediment was not without its difficulties. Educators discouraged me from considering higher education, and others often laughed at me because I had difficulties articulating fluently and coherently. What I say to that now is, "But God." With each step, I learned to rely more on God's strength and less on my own. This resilience enabled me to continue speaking, even when I faced obstacles, knowing that God's grace was sufficient for every situation.

Lessons we can learn from Isaiah 41:10 as it connects with "Eating Fear for Breakfast" that fear can often feel like a formidable foe. However, when we choose to eat fear for breakfast by facing it with faith, empowerment, assurance, and resilience, we can transform it from a hindrance into a stepping stone. Isaiah 41:10 serves as a powerful reminder that we do not face our fears alone. God is with us; he strengthens us; he helps us, and he upholds us with his righteous right hand.

So, the next time you feel fear creeping in, remember that you have the power to overcome it. With God by your side, you can face any challenge with confidence, knowing that he is your strength and support. Embrace fear as an opportunity to grow in faith and resilience, and trust that God will carry you through every situation. Eat fear for breakfast, and let it fuel your journey of faith.

Let's Pray

Thank you, God, for your unwavering presence and strength in our lives. As we face our fears, remind us of the promises in Isaiah 41:10: God is with us; God will strengthen us, help us, and uphold us with his righteous right hand. Grant us the faith to trust in God's power, the empowerment to act with courage, the assurance of God's unfailing support, and the resilience to overcome any obstacle. Help us to embrace our fears as opportunities to grow closer to you and to walk boldly in the path that God has set before us.

In Jesus' name, we pray.

Amen

Journal

What is God speaking to you?

About Dr. Sanja

Recognized as a thought leader, Dr. Sanja Rickette Stinson brings over four decades of invaluable experience as the founding CEO of Matthew House - Chicago, a supportive service center for the homeless. Raised by entrepreneurial parents, Gus and Mary Rickette, Dr. Sanja carries forward a legacy of leadership and innovation.

Dr. Sanja is the president of Empower Her Ventures, LLC, and founder of Dr. Sanja Coaching & Consulting, where she is dedicated to transforming the lives of faith-based and professional women over the age of 50.

Her mission is to empower these women to embrace their roles as disruptors, encouraging them to reframe and reimagine their lives with a focus on self-care and rejuvenation.

Beyond her nonprofit leadership, Dr. Sanja is a certified coach, business strategist, speaker, best-selling author, blogger, and ordained minister. Through these channels, she inspires individuals to unlock their leadership potential and pursue personal growth. Her best-selling anthology trilogy collection, "Disrupting the Status Quo," underscores her commitment to visionary leadership, ministry, and community development. This dedication has amplified her impact globally, making her a sought-after speaker at international conferences and events. She has also co-authored works such as "Trailblazers 2," "Possibilities Unlimited," and "Dare to Rise Above Mediocrity" alongside renowned figures like Les Brown and Dr. Cheryl Wood.

Dr. Sanja served as the founding pastor of Victory & Grace Christian Church and was commissioned as an apostle in 2018. She has ordained ministers and currently serves as the pastor emeritus of Victory & Grace Christian Church. Her academic journey includes degrees from DePaul University, McCormick Theological Seminary, Concordia University and Northern Theological Seminary. Dr. Sanja's relentless pursuit of excellence shows no signs of abating.

For those seeking to connect with her, inquiries can be directed to:

Website: drsanja.com

Email: info@drsanja.com.

Today's Scripture

And Jesus said to him, If you can! All things are possible for one who believes.

Mark 9:23

Day 2

MY PATH TO WRITING AND HEALING

By Donna Izzard

We often hesitate to make moves because of our inner fears. When we understand who we are in Christ and choose to believe in him alone, everything changes. I remember when the Lord instructed me to write my first book. I hesitated, fearful of what he was asking me to share. What would people think if I told my truth? I was fearful of how my family would react and how my church family would respond. Despite my fears, I knew I needed to write the book because it would be both liberating and healing. Fear can be paralyzing, convincing us to stay silent and stagnant. I came up with numerous reasons not to proceed, but I also knew that disobeying God's assignment would not be good for me. I understood that many women would find deliverance and freedom through my testimony. Yet, fear held me back.

One day, I attended a workshop and met a literary agent. I shared my book outline with her, and she encouraged me to write my story. As I began to pray and read God's promises, I felt encouraged to write. With each word, the chains of fear started to break away from me. I stood on God's word, believing that he had brought me through my experiences to give him glory and to help other women in similar situations. Writing became a path to freedom for both me and those who would read my book.

Mark 9:23 says, "And Jesus said to him, 'If you can! All things are possible for one who believes.'" This verse resonated deeply with me during this journey. It reminded me that by believing in Jesus, all things are possible. My fears, though strong, were no match for the power of faith in Christ. This scripture encouraged me to move forward, trusting that God's purpose for my story would be fulfilled and that my testimony would bring hope and healing to others.

God kept speaking to me; I had to write this book. I could not let the emotion of fear grip me. I had to make a decision that writing the book was of him and not of fear. Fear would be a distraction if I allowed it to consume me. He directed me to his Word, and I found strength and encouragement there.

Another scripture that greatly encouraged me is 2 Timothy 1:7: "For God has not given us a spirit of fear, but of power and of love and of a sound mind." This promise reminded me that fear is not from God. He gives us the power to overcome it, the love to move forward, and the sound mind to carry out his will. This assurance gave me the courage to write my book and share my testimony, knowing that God was with me every step of the way.

Let's Pray

Father, in the name of Jesus, I ask that you transform the hearts of those reading this chapter. Replace their fear with your divine courage and help them to trust fully in your promises. Fill them wIth the power of your love and grant them a sound mind to carry out the purpose you have for their lives. May they step out in faith, knowing that with you, all things are possible.

In Jesus' name,

Amen

EAT FEAR FOR BREAKFAST

Journal

What is God speaking to you?

About Donna

Donna Izzard is a distinguished leader, coach and speaker, recognized for her significant contributions to professional development. Named by the "Huffington Post" as one of the top coaches to watch, Donna has consistently demonstrated excellence in her field. She was also honored by "Impact Magazine" as one of 30 Black Global Leaders, a recognition that highlights her dedication to empowering, encouraging and educating others through powerful imagery and storytelling.

As an entrepreneur and best-selling author, Donna has successfully launched and managed her own *business while also serving as one of the few women technology training directors at an AmLaw100 law firm. Her 30-plus years in corporate America have honed her God-given gift for innovation and her remarkable ability to bring out the inner, often hidden, phenomenal in people.*

Donna's achievements were further acknowledged when she was selected as a Notable Black Leader by "Crain's New York Business" publication. This prestigious honor celebrates her outstanding professional and community achievements, which have greatly enhanced New York City and the lives of its inhabitants. Donna continues to inspire and drive meaningful change, making her a vital asset to her organization and the broader community.

EAT FEAR FOR BREAKFAST

Today's Scripture

Peace I leave with you; my peace I give to you. Not as the world gives you do I give to you. Let not your hearts be troubled, neither let them be afraid.

John 14:27

Day 3

GET MOVING

By Liz Hoop

Have you ever moved away from all that was familiar to you — your friends, family, town or city and job? When the Lord told me it was time to let go of where I was and to move, I fought it. I didn't want to leave the familiar. I didn't want to give up the life I had and move to a place where the only people I did know was my immediate family. But all the doors where I was started slamming in my face, making it clear it was time to go.

For two years, my family (specifically one sister) encouraged me to make the move closer to them, as I lived almost 500 miles away. I packed up my home and moved back to my home state where I didn't have any friends or business associates, just my family. I knew I would need to meet people once I got moved, so I began doing what I know best, which is getting out and meeting people.

Even though I'm good at meeting people, I admit that at first, I was a little tentative; however, I started going to social networking gatherings. I bought a home, which put me near the church I now call my church home. God placed godly people in my life to help me build my relationship with him. I learned I had to walk by faith when I felt him leading me in unexpected places. The one thing I knew was that if I wanted to feel peace, I had to be obedient to his leadership. Getting out there, stepping out of my comfort zone so many times, speaking on platforms I would not ever have been on had I not been obedient, and serving in organizations whose missions are my heart — all led me to know a peace unlike any I had known.

Let's Pray

Abba Father,

Thanks for the peace you give me when I'm walking into the unknown, the peace that comes from knowing you're walking with me, the peace in knowing that you'll direct my steps and guide me in the direction you have chosen for me.

Amen

Journal

What is God speaking to you?

About Liz

Liz Hoop, multi-time international best-selling author, is the owner and CEO of Hoop Cares LLC, a senior concierge business providing transportation and in-home caregiving services. She loves helping and encouraging others; she finds it her calling and a way to minister to others. She attends Magnolia Springs church, where she a leader of the women's ministry team. She serves on the board of directors for the Mental Health Association of South Mississippi,

Adult & Teen Challenge for Women in Mississippi and WOW - Women of Wisdom. She serves as the chairperson for TRIAD of Jackson County, Miss., an organization that works to continually improve safety awareness education among senior citizens. She's also a community educator for the Alzheimer's Association of MS. Liz selflessly gives of her time in volunteer efforts that help others. Liz has received numerous nominations and awards recognizing all her efforts. She was recently named one of the 100 Successful Women to Know for 2024 and was a Best Of Mississippi Award winner; she was named Author of Anthology for the Year and was recognized with the award for Small Business Owner of Hoop Cares LLC.

Connect with Liz via Facebook – www.facebook.com/lizhoop
These accomplishments stand as a testament to the profound impact of faith and the unwavering guidance of the Lord.

Ethel may be reached at ethelpolite24@gmail.com and www.joyinhopeministries.com.

EAT FEAR FOR BREAKFAST

Today's Scripture

*Blessed is everyone who fears the Lord, who walks in his ways! You shall eat the fruit of the labor of your hands; you shall be blessed,
and it shall be well with you.*

Psalm 128:1-2

Day 4

EMBRACE FAITH: FLOURISH WITHOUT FEAR

By Jai Cornell

Having survived this earth for half a century, I have learned that happiness is not something to be derived from without — only from within. I struggled with fear of the unknown, of what I couldn't accomplish, of dreams going sour and refusing to come to fruition. I was left with regret thinking about the past and with sorrow for that which could not be changed. So, to slay the three Fs — fear, falter and forgetting, I decided to take a break from life.

When I remember with appreciation my past and the transformation that I have been through, with the efforts I had to make to survive at different times of my life, all I feel is fire inside me, which burns, stirs me up to want and attempt to do something to give, and bring my faith to as many people as possible. If I walk in the Word of the Lord, and if I have the strength to leave my preoccupations behind, I have faith to understand that the Lord will guide me to wellness, goodness to prosperity, too.

Reaching 50 is to enter an era of cherishing life, to bear witness to faith and hard work. It inspires me every day to walk by faith, not by sight, so that with the Lord I might be caught in feet first when I step into eternity and to help others to flourish in life without regrets. Happiness for me comes now by being at peace and at joy with the God who has called me to himself to be fruitful and multiply!

Let's Pray

Dear Lord,

Thank you, Lord, for leading us and for helping us to trust you in all our ways. We seek to continue to walk in you and find our place in your script — please take our grief and worry and allow that fire that you have given to shine out from us that others may continue to walk in faith and find purpose. Bless our work and labor and let our journeys speak to others to continue to walk in faith.

Amen

Journal

What is God speaking to you?

About Jai

Jai Cornell is coach, facilitator, author, speaker, servant leader and publisher encouraging people to share their stories in the "Permission to Flourish" anthology series. A four-time Amazon best-selling author, Jai leads global talent development across multiple industries. Jai Cornell launched her "PTF" (Permission to Flourish) magazine globally on June 1, 2024, resulting from 18 months of work to be published.

Outside of her professional endeavors, Jai

contributed extensively to philanthropy and community service while leveraging her expert knowledge to foster a culture of encouragement, better opportunities and well-being. As a storyteller, author and entrepreneur, she actively seeks to find accessible avenues to foster brand growth. She strongly believes our stories shape the changing landscape of the world because within a story lies the power to impact the mind of an individual.

Facebook: https://www.facebook.com/yiayiacornell

EAT FEAR FOR BREAKFAST

Today's Scripture

Fear not, for I am with you; be not dismayed, for I am your God; I will strengthen you, I will help you, I will uphold you with my righteous right hand.

Isaiah 41:10

Day 5

FEAR WHAT? HELD IN HIS RIGHT HAND

By Lillian Harrison

Life has a way of presenting challenges when we least expect them, often testing our resilience and faith. For me, this truth came crashing down in a doctor's office after a simple fall escalated into a diagnosis of osteoarthritis. The words from the doctor felt like a stark revelation of my physical limitations: "You have osteoarthritis," he said. "It's not reversible."

Suddenly, aging became an undeniable reality. I noticed it in the little things — getting up slower, needing to stretch before taking a step. Despite my efforts, some days the pain was almost unbearable, especially after long days spent serving others, like distributing food to the hungry or walking through the confines of a prison. My inflamed knees protested, reminding me of their irreversible condition.

In these moments of physical strain and despair, when fear whispered that my days of activity might be numbered, Isaiah 41:10 echoed powerfully in my heart. "Fear not, for I am with you." This promise became my lifeline. God did not say I would not face physical pain or limitations, but he assured me of his unceasing presence and support.

God's promise to uphold us with his right hand is not just about spiritual support; it extends to our physical trials as well. The days when pain flares up and the body cries out for rest, these are the times when his words take on a deeper significance. It's a reminder that our strength does not come from our physical capabilities but from the one who promises to help and uphold us.

For anyone struggling with chronic pain or facing the daunting prospects of aging, the fear of what tomorrow might bring can be overwhelming. Yet, God invites us to lean into his eternal strength and righteousness. He asks us not to dwell on our fears but to trust in his steadfast presence and unfailing help.

Let's Pray

Heavenly Father,

In our moments of physical pain and weakness, when our bodies fail us and our spirits falter, remind us of your promise to never leave us nor forsake us. Help us to not fear our limitations or the challenges of aging, but to embrace your strength as sufficient for every pain and every trial.

Thank you for the assurance that you are with us, strengthening us, helping us and upholding us with your righteous right hand. On days when the pain seems too much to bear, let this promise be our comfort and our motivation to keep moving forward.

Grant us the courage to continue serving and loving others, knowing that you will provide the strength we need for each day. May we always remember that we do not walk alone, for you are our God, our strength and our ever-present help.

In your holy name, we pray,

Amen

Journal

What is God speaking to you?

About Lillian

Lillian Harrison is a dynamic leader and advocate, known for her multifaceted roles in the community. She is the founder and executive director of Elevated Community Development Corporation, an organization dedicated to providing training, employment and support to prior offenders, veterans and the homeless. Elevated CDC also mentors the next generation, dubbed Motivated Millennials, in life skills, financial literacy, and entrepreneurship.

Lillian is a full-time pastor at Elevated Ministries, collaborating with local churches and community organizations to develop programs and services tailored to the needs of congregations and communities. In addition to her pastoral work, she is a licensed real estate agent and the owner of a women's empowerment boutique offering apparel, jewelry, and fragrances.

Her empowerment initiatives extend further through her coaching program, Purpose Over Pain, and her authorship of several publications. As executive director of Independent Resources Inc., Lillian is also actively involved in mentoring entrepreneurs with disabilities. She holds various leadership roles, including serving on the executive committee for Sussex County Economic Development Action Committee, the Advisory Board of Delaware Botanical Gardens, the Governor's Council on Housing and the Delaware Community Reinvestment Action Council.

With a mission to empower and uplift, Lillian continues to make a significant impact through her various professional and community engagements.

Lillian may be reached at elevatedcdc@gmail.com.

EAT FEAR FOR BREAKFAST

Today's Scripture

Look at the birds of the air: they neither sow nor reap nor gather into barns, and yet your heavenly Father feeds them. Are you not of more value.

Matthew 6:26

EAT FEAR FOR BREAKFAST

Day 6

I AM NOT BROKE

By Monica Lloyd

I find it interesting that God created animals before creating the man, Adam. He made sure all things were available for the animals to feast from in water and on land. There was nothing they were lacking and were fulfilled in this new place. Yet somehow as we live life, we think something is missing, and our self-gratifications are not being satisfied, which then makes us flow into thinking that God does not care. It seems like he keeps us on the edge, then boom! He shows up.

I recall a song by Lynn Anderson titled, "I Never Promised You A Rose Garden." The lyrics said, "Along with the sunshine, there's going to be a little rain sometimes," and if you are one who focuses on the rain, you are missing out on the beautiful sunshine. It is both the sunshine and rain that produce a nice fragrance in your life. It took me awhile to figure that out. My focus was all off. The rain and thunderstorms got more of my attention. Why wasn't I being taken care of like the creatures in the garden were? Whatever they needed was provided, and they wanted for nothing.

I had to take a step back out of my own life to get a different view. I feared lack — not having enough — and this caused me to not sow with a cheerful heart. It made me hold back my tithes to be ready for those just-in-case scenarios — you know, those unexpected bills, car trouble, going out with friends, and such. Lack was something I experienced throughout my childhood. My mom would say that she was always robbing Peter to pay Paul, and I felt so sorry for Peter. From my perspective, it seemed that money was always short.

It was not until my adulthood and until I had a personal relationship with God that I began to see how we were taken care of through the processes of our journey; our minds were still intact; we still had physical abilities (to some degree for some), and my mom kept the faith and still loved God.

As it is with parents, so is it with your heavenly Father. He is not going to give you all your soul's desires, but he will provide the necessities of life and some earthly treasures. As I learned stewardship, my mindset began to change. Money or lack of it was not the problem; it was my trust in the supplier.

I came to understand that I am important to God, and he makes sure daily that his children have what is sufficient. Matthew 6:11 states, "Give us today our daily bread." You cannot allow your thoughts to stretch so far out beyond tomorrow, for your needs will be taken care of. Just know this: God takes care of the fowls of the air, and he will take care of you, every day.

Let's Pray

Father God,

I trust you to take care of me. I lack for nothing, and all my needs are met through Christ Jesus. You are my resource for the necessities in my life. I am loved and well taken care of. In Jesus' name.

Amen

Journal

What is God speaking to you?

About Monica

Monica Lloyd is a woman with an apostolic teaching anointing who can discern the intents of the heart of mankind and bring deliverance through her teachings with the clarity of God's Word. Feeding souls is her mission, helping to bring about complete wholeness through Jesus Christ.

She currently serves as the executive pastor of Unveiled Ministries of Chicago, Ill., under the senior leadership of Apostle Sharon R. Peters-Ruff.

Monica has been in ministry for over 20 years, and her coming into the knowledge of the Lord Jesus Christ has brought her great fulfillment in life as she walks out his plans. She knows that desires without Christ are only self-willed ambitions.

Being in union with her husband, George Lloyd, for 37 years and being a mother of three sons and grandmother to eight children, she has been shown that her that marriage can yet be blissful and fulfilling. She sincerely believes that when God is made the anchor, there will be no uprooting!

How to contact Monica:

Facebook: Dr. Monica Lloyd

EAT FEAR FOR BREAKFAST

EAT FEAR FOR BREAKFAST

Today's Scripture

But when Jesus heard it he said, "This illness does not lead to death. It is for the glory of God, so that the Son of God may be glorified through it."

John 11:41

Day 7

MISTAKES

By Monique Mitchell

The Mayo Clinic doctor's words still ring in my ears: "You have multiple sclerosis."

I was extremely afraid. Was my life ending at the early age of 39? I had so many plans and dreams to realize.

Then came the doctor's bleak prognosis: "The best we can hope for is keeping you out of a wheelchair before the age of 50." There is no cure for MS. I felt the urgent need to get my house in order! The clock was ticking; I was running out of time.

I wondered whether I had asked forgiveness from everyone and anyone I might have hurt or wronged. I wondered whether my relationship with God was up to par. I considered my loved ones. Whom should I tell? So many unknowns left unimaginable feat at my doorstep.

Although I had accomplished a great deal in just 39 years, I felt my life was just beginning. I had been married only 9 years and had been in the house of my dreams for only 8 years. I needed God to show me how he would be glorified by this situation.

As the disease progressed, I developed optic neuritis and severe vertigo and committed to walking with a walker. I felt nearly helpless. Being stripped of my independence, I was running out of options, I began to hear the Spirit of the Lord say, "You are living to live." Each day, I anticipated that God's miraculous hand would prove me to be a living testimony of his great grace and plentiful mercy. Faith carried me.

Yes, this has been hard a hard cup to drink from. I have learned to make both spiritual and physical life adjustments. But God has been there every step of the way. My relationship with God has grown and flourished. I now depend on God for everything! This sickness is not until death. But until then, I am living a life closer to God. I'm glorifying God with praise because I'm a living masterpiece of what he can do in one's life. I now have access to all of the amazing medical advancements God has given to the MS community, and I live a fruitful and full life through Jesus Christ.

Let's Pray

Father

I thank you that we don't have to fear when we are confronted with illnesses because you will get the glory, as it is a testament of our faith, and all we need to do is trust in you.

Amen!

Journal

What is God speaking to you?

EAT FEAR FOR BREAKFAST

About Monique

Monique Mitchell is an intercessor who says she finds complete joy when praying for others. After attending UCLA and working for more than 25 years in hospital administration, she now devotes her life and time to ministry. She has managed the I Am Strong ministry since 2020. At 56, Monque says she is "beyond blessed that my life is just beginning as I complete my assignment for the Kingdom of God!"

Monique may be reached at m.monique1@gmail.com.

EAT FEAR FOR BREAKFAST

Today's Scripture

*Remember not the former things, nor consider things of the old. Behold, I am doing a new thing; now it springs forth. Do you not perceive it?
I will make a way in the wilderness and rivers in the desert.*

Isaiah 43:18-19

Day 8

DON'T LOOK BACK!

By Ravyn Hill

Fear of inadequacy, failure, and success gripped me all at once. I was a mother of one and expecting another when life's major storm took place in my home. I was on the brink of divorce, on maternity leave, had a broken leg, and was battling constant abuse. I found myself in a place of pity and disbelief. How could I be in this position?

God pointed me back to the day I'd said, "Yes", to a man and no to Him. Raised in the church all my life, I desired to see what was beyond the walls of the sanctuary. "Surely, there has to be more to life than this," I'd said to myself. I wanted everything that was opposite of God so that I could really experience all the world had to offer.

I made this decision out of lust, curiosity and immaturity. I'd soon regret it and crawl on my face back to the Great I Am!

God saw what I couldn't see and sent warnings to me through my dreams; he'd literally speak with an audible voice of the things I was not to partake of. My flesh would take precedence.

I'd spend many years in torment that left me feeling less and less valuable, inadequate, incapable and fearful. Many times, I'd cry and scream out loud to God, "I need you, Lord!"

He heard me! He rescued me! He'd given me a gift that birthed in me courage, grace, peace and restoration. With this new-found boldness and perspective on the things God was doing, I'd somehow become unable to shake a new fear: fear of being successful.

I'd given birth to my baby girl, escaped and divorced my husband, survived every day's challenges and regained some self-confidence. What if I become too good "on my own?" Will God no longer hear me? Will all my success be taken away? For we know God is attracted to our dependency on him. If I continue to do well, will my abuser return? I was tormented by thoughts planted by the enemy. I'd say to myself, "You're not yet healed from all the trauma, so I know I'm going to self-sabotage all these good things."

In my moment of panic, God showed me his promise: "But seek first the kingdom of God and his righteousness, and all these things will be added to you." (Matthew 6:33)

This day would take years to achieve, but through prayer and the prayers of others, I'd see God's promises come to fruition. Behold, he makes all things new. Do not consider your past or the place from where you have come, but acknowledge that the God of all grace and mercies has you in mind and promises to restore you. Keep your eyes on Christ Jesus, and he will truly direct your path. You are fearfully and wonderfully made. Peace and prosperity are your portions. I declare that I am an overcomer.

God has given me a personal escort out of the city!

Let's Pray

Lord,

   We thank you for your promises and your word that will never return to you void. You have kept us in the valley, sheltered us from the storms and covered us with your mighty wing. You have given us a way out -- out of bondage, fears, deserts, wilderness and pits. You are faithful and just. Your only desire is that we surrender all to you. Today, Lord, we lay it all at your feet and fix our eyes on you. I bind the temptation to look back and accept your grace to move forward. I will seek you first in all things.

   Amen

… EAT FEAR FOR BREAKFAST

Journal

What is God speaking to you?

About Ravyn

Ravyn Hill is a giver, mother and friend. Her greatest joy comes from serving others and putting smiles on the hearts of all she encounters. Her ministries include choreographing praise dances, singing and serving all those in need. She is a survivor of domestic and narcissistic abuse who strives daily to do the will of God and live for his glory alone.

Ravyn may be reached at ravyn.hill@yahoo.com.

EAT FEAR FOR BREAKFAST

Today's Scripture

And after you have suffered a little while, the God of all grace, who has called you to his eternal glory in Christ, will himself restore, confirm, strengthen and establish you.

1 Peter 5:10

Day 9

YOU'RE AN OVERCOMER!

By Ravyn Hill

Trials and tribulations — we all go through them; some are harsher than others.

I exchanged my identity in Christ for an identity in man and was left in the wilderness alone and afraid, screaming out loud for God to rescue me.

I'd soon understand that he never left me; it was I who left him. Clinging to Christ as if I were taking my last breath, I'd hear his voice saying: "Now is the time for necessary endings." (Ecclesiastes 3:1-8).

Sanity was nowhere to be found; desires were lost; self-worth was demolished, and I began to wonder what I was to become, if anything, and where I was to go, if anywhere. I had surrendered my being to a man and got nothing but turmoil in return. I thought, "Lord, if you will help me get through this, I will never turn away from you again." He again reminded me that I had to let go of the idols that I had placed ahead of him.

As I surrendered, the Lord began to dismantle the altars I had unconsciously built and to open the ears and eyes of my spirit. I began to realize I am stronger, wiser, and more valuable — clothed in my right mind, full of peace and happiness with Christ. My fears began to fall away, one by one, and boldness crept in. My armor was impenetrable, and my head was now anointed. I knew then that I could do all things through Christ who strengthened me. I was and am a conqueror. I am an overcomer!

Let's Pray

Dear Lord,

Thank you, Lord, for leading us and for helping us to trust you in all our ways. We seek to continue to walk in you and find our place in your script — please take our grief and worry and allow that fire that you have given to shine out from us that others may continue to walk in faith and find purpose. Bless our work and labor and let our journeys speak to others to continue to walk in faith.

Amen

Journal

What is God speaking to you?

About Ravyn

Ravyn Hill is a giver, mother and friend. Her greatest joy comes from serving others and putting smiles on the hearts of all she encounters. Her ministries include choreographing praise dances, singing and serving all those in need. She is a survivor of domestic and narcissistic abuse who strives daily to do the will of God and live for his glory alone.

Ravyn may be reached at ravyn.hill@yahoo.com.

Today's Scripture

For I know the plans that I have for you, declares the Lord, plans for welfare and not for evil, to give you a future and hope.

Jeremiah 29:11

Day 10

KEPT AND COVERED

By Shalette Persaud

What happens when your life and plans get abruptly and suddenly interrupted, and your foundation gets shaken beyond your control? Or your vision gets distorted because deceit and betrayal enter the room and try to find a seat at your table? When you look around and find you can no longer trust any of the people you cared deeply about? When you can't trust their words, motives, actions or even their presence? That is what happened to me, but little did I realize that God had greater plans and places for me.

The Lord introduced himself to me in such a way that I will never forget that I can trust him; I will never doubt that he is true to his word and that he alone is faithful. He showed me that he would protect, provide and prepare through his word. He told me that it was time to take my eyes and ears off of the people I could no longer trust — despite the anger, the lies, the evil, the warfare and the disappointment — so I could hear him and obey. I had to go on a faith walk.

He first came to me in a quiet voice by giving me a scripture. He spoke out to me randomly, giving me the scripture Jeremiah 29:11 while I was going down the aisles picking up fans after a church service. I heard him, but didn't respond; I just thought, "Jeremiah?"

He again called out the same scripture: "Jeremiah 29:11," this time with a little more urgency.

I responded "Okay, Lord, I will look for it when I finish."

At the time I wasn't familiar with that scripture; I wasn't aware of what it said or even sure if it was actually in the Bible. Well clearly, he heard my thoughts and shouted at me, "JEREMIAH 29:11!" ... in other words, hurry up and find it!

Through this scripture, he personally revealed himself and invited me to trust him — trust him, and believe before I knew what was going to happen.

We have a Father who knows us so intimately that he already knows how we will respond as his children. He had to get to my mind before the enemy could get to my ear. He called out to me, and I knew his voice. He was going to have a personal encounter with me. The plan was to show me that he is in control and that whatever the enemy meant for evil, he was able to use for his good. He wanted to use me as his vessel.

Before you execute your agenda, the Lord says, I'm going to impart my agenda. I'm going to arrest your thoughts and adjust them to my plan. I'm going to teach you to trust me wholeheartedly without doubt or compromise. I am going to teach you how to prepare for my plan. I am going to personally equip you. I am going to teach you to be my intercessor. But first you have to come and pray.

The Lord kept reminding me: "I know the thoughts that I think towards you. It's what I say that matters. Come up higher. I have a place and provision for you."

The Lord had to take me through the fire on many levels. I had to be tested so that I could be refined. Through the years, despite what I faced, even today, all I can hear is the Lord saying, "I have plans for you."

He heals the heart, heals the hurt, heals the pain, heals the shame; he heals the past. Know that the Lord has good plans for you. You will get your vision back and see so clearly how the Lord has watched over you. You may be in a foreign place, but the Lord says he will take care of you.

Let's Pray

Heavenly Father,

Thank you for showing me that I can trust your plans and thoughts towards me. You protect me and are true to your word concerning me. Thank you for allowing me to hear your voice so that I can obey. Thank you for reminding me that I have an abundant eternal future with you.

Amen

Journal

What is God speaking to you?

_____

_____

_____

_____

_____

_____

_____

_____

_____

_____

_____

_____

_____

_____

_____

_____

_____

_____

_____

_____

About Shalette

Shalette Persaud has a genuine gift of encouragement, motivation and inspiration to help others know that with God, they can overcome anything that is set before them. She says, "There is no problem too hard for him, and you can do nothing without him!"

Shalette is a committed mother of four young adult children. She holds a posture of humility, honor, loyalty and grace with a sincere love for God's people and the Kingdom. She is often reading, involved in a Bible study or on a prayer line. She enjoys a good road trip, vacation and understands the importance of self-care.

Shalette serves as a ministry leader at Temple Baptist Church in Long Beach, Calif. She serves as a ministry coordinator with Abounding Love Bible Ministry, moderator/host/exhorter of "TikTalk Tuesday" with Abounding Love Bible Ministry; and an exhorter with Bishop Sean Teal on National Prayer Call

You can connect with Shalette via:

jaemae2000@yahoo.com
SPersaud@albministry.org
Facebook

Today's Scripture

*There is no fear in love,
but perfect love casts out fear.*

I John 4:18

Day 11

WHAT'S LOVE GOT TO DO WITH IT?

By Sheila D. Reynolds

When I was born again, I immediately sensed a calling to lead. My passion for God's Word led me to spend countless hours reading, praying and studying. However, I struggled with fears and insecurities. I didn't fully understand my identity in Christ and would often feel inadequate. Watching others teach and lead, I felt God urging me to step forward, but fear of the unfamiliar, criticism and vulnerability held me back. Each time God prompted me to speak, I retreated, fearing failure. My desire for perfection and approval from others kept me stuck in fear.

One day, during prayer, God revealed to me that I was in the way, that I was placing too much focus on me and not him. He wasn't concerned whether I was perfect. He wasn't concerned about how I came across to others — I was. He wanted my obedience to be to him, not to the standard of excellence I held myself to. I was reminded of the scripture in John 14:15: "If you love me, you will keep my commandments." I was also reminded of I John 4:18, which says that perfect love casts out fear. I realized that if I really love God and the people he's called me to serve, that this perfect love has the power to break me free from fear. Whew! It was a powerful revelation and shift for me when I realized that I was focused more on my comfort than I was on pleasing God. I was in fear because I wanted to be accepted by others. I didn't want to experience criticism and failure. I denied others the healing, deliverance and transformation that God equipped me to bring because of my self-centeredness and fear.

To combat my fears, I began daily meditating on scriptures and turning them into personal declarations. I declared 2 Timothy 1:7: "God did not give me the spirit of fear, but of power, love, and a sound mind." As I studied and internalized this and other scriptures, I began to see an authentic boldness arise in me. I started developing confidence and began setting goals to intentionally push myself out of my comfort zone. I began to activate my faith by obeying God in taking small steps without fully understanding the bigger picture.

When I moved to Savannah, Ga., in 2011, God instructed me to gather women for prayer. Despite feeling alone, unsure, and not knowing many people, I obeyed. I started praying every Friday night at 7 p.m. Initially, it was just me, but I was obedient and consistent. This led to hosting a women's prayer breakfast and later an all-night prayer event. As I continued to follow God's guidance, I began a teaching and prayer ministry, a coaching and mentoring group which has become a thriving women's empowerment community. At each step, I focused on my love for God and those I'm called to serve. I discovered that perfect love does indeed cast out fear. I encourage you to let God's perfect love cast out your fear and propel you into the purpose he has for you.

Let's Pray

Heavenly Father,

Thank you for your perfect love that casts out all fear. Help us shift our focus from ourselves to you, trusting your guidance and embracing your call. Fill us with courage and boldness to serve with joy and confidence. Guide us every step, and let your love lead us into your purpose. In Jesus' name we pray.

Amen

Journal

What is God speaking to you?

About Sheila

Sheila Reynolds is a licensed professional counselor, board-certified coach and founder of Wake Up, Rise Up, Live Up, a movement that is jolting women into an awakening of who they are called to be. But really, she is the sister-friend that every woman needs to help her ascend to the next level of her life. Through annual conferences, book collaboration projects, intimate retreats and Christian coaching programs, she empowers women to break free from limitations and *boldly embrace their unique purpose and design.*

In 2019, Sheila established The BLOOM Project, a sacred sisterhood of successful women dedicated to transforming lives by sharing their personal stories. These authentic and transparent stories are published yearly and provide a road map to true love, freedom and fulfillment.

In 2023, Sheila established Born to Flourish, a faith-based membership community for women over 50 who are rediscovering, redefining and rejuvenating their lives.

For over 30 years, Sheila has devoted her life to empowering and uplifting women. She has mentored and coached hundreds of young women, many of whom have become successful teachers, entrepreneurs, counselors, social workers and ministers.

You may connect with Sheila at www.borntoflourishnetwork.com

Today's Scripture

Have I not commanded you? Be strong and courageous. Do not be afraid; do not be discouraged, for the Lord your God will be with you wherever you go.

Joshua 1:9

Day 12

WAKE UP A FAITH-BURNING LIONESS

By Starr Chapman

On a Friday night, after returning home from work, I sat on the sofa drinking my customary two glasses of wine. I was feeling hollow, bored and empty. I had lost my faith, and without faith there is no hope, and there was none.

And then I heard something, a voice. I looked around the house, but I was still alone. It said, "Is this how you are going out?" What??? Then, more forcefully: "Is this how you are going to go out?" I froze, not because of the voice but because of the question. Was this how I was going to go out? Was this all that my life was going to amount to? No! Absolutely not!

I went into the bathroom to splash some water on my face, and hanging on the rod was an embroidered tea towel that my daughter had given to me. The words on it read, "Be Strong and

Courageous" — Joshua. Talk about the right words at the right time.

Since that time, I have awakened every morning thanking God for that revelation and the strength to continue to work to bring people together.

Let's Pray

Heavenly Father,

Thank you for this beautiful gift of life and the many lives that we touch every day. Let our hearts not be saddened but lifted to emanate your glory and love for all of us.

Amen

Journal

What is God speaking to you?

EAT FEAR FOR BREAKFAST

About Starr

Starr Chapman has been a restaurateur on the Gulf Coast for 40 years. During that time, she created and worked on many fundraisers across the Coast. Because of her extensive networking and connections, Attorney General Lynn Fitch tapped Starr to join her team as a Constituent Outreach Officer. Today, Starr travels around the state of Mississippi, connecting and networking with charities, business owners, Rotarians, *government officials and many others to assist in building stronger communities for all Mississippians.*

You can reach Starr at starrchapman7@gmail.com.

EAT FEAR FOR BREAKFAST

EAT FEAR FOR BREAKFAST

Today's Scripture

Do not be anxious about anything, but in everything by prayer and supplication with thanksgiving let your requests be made known to God.
And the peace of God, which surpasses all understanding, will guard your hearts and your minds in Christ Jesus.

Philippians 4:6-7

Day 13

WHEN FEAR CALLED, FAITH ANSWERED

By Teri Riley

I received the call that every woman dreads. My doctor informed me that my routine test had come back abnormal, and a biopsy was necessary. My heart sank.

The days leading up to the biopsy dragged on like an eternity. Each day felt heavier than the last. I couldn't shake the fear of the unknown, and worry consumed my thoughts. I was a mother, and thoughts of not being around for my children weighed heavily on my mind. But through it all, I clung to my faith.

Every morning, I prayed for strength and peace, finding reassurance in knowing God was with me. Without him, I would have lost my mind. That unwavering faith became my anchor, guiding me through the uncertainty and fear. I reached out to my tribe, who surrounded me with incredible love and support and prayed to God for complete healing and total restoration.

When the biopsy results came back, my doctor said I had abnormal cells that would develop into cancer. He said that I needed surgery. Instead of fear, I felt a deep sense of acceptance because I knew God had my back. I trusted in his plan and leaned on my faith.

The surgery was a success, and miraculously, it revealed no evidence of the initial diagnosis of abnormal cells! God had answered our prayers and restored me. I now know without a shadow of a doubt that nothing is too hard for God. His power and love carried me through my darkest moments, turning fear into faith and despair into hope. This experience has deepened my belief that with God, all things are possible. I am forever grateful for His miraculous healing in my life. May I be a living testimony to his goodness, sharing with all who need a dose of hope.

Let's Pray

Father God,

   We come before you today with hearts full of gratitude, despite our fears. Thank you for your unwavering love and kindness that give us strength in our moments of anxiety. Your faithfulness has been our anchor through every challenge, guiding us with your comforting presence.

   Help us, Lord, to live each day in thankfulness for the courage and peace you've brought into our lives. Let our actions and words reflect your grace and power to those around us. Allow our light to shine so others can see you in us and be inspired to trust in your unfailing love, even in the face of fear.

In Jesus' name,

Amen

Journal

What is God speaking to you?

About Teri

Teri Riley is a certified image consultant, personal stylist and speaker dedicated to the empowerment of women and girls. She believes all are uniquely beautiful and created with value and purpose.

Teri has always had a passion for fashion for more than 11 years has been a personal stylist for a women's clothing company where she helps her clients express their unique strengths and beauty through fashion.

She is the founder and CEO of Empowered Styles,

which helps women discover their unique personal style and offers personal branding, closet sessions and shopping services for women.

She is a No. 1 best-selling author on Amazon, having released her first book, "Moms Who Boss Up Post Pandemic: Successful Moms Who Pivoted to Success in the Face Of Uncertainty," a collaboration with 15 other moms.

She is happily married, has three children and continues to spend her free time learning and experimenting with clothes and accessories, exercising her unlimited creativity in the world of fashion and self-expression.

For those seeking to connect with her, inquiries can be directed to:

Website: www.empoweredstyles.com

Email: teri@empoweredstyles.com

LinkedIn: https://www.linkedin.com/in/teri-riley-52b26418/

Instagram: https://www.instagram.com/stylishlyteri

EAT FEAR FOR BREAKFAST

Today's Scripture

Be strong and courageous; do not fear or be in dread of them, for it is the Lord your God who goes with you. He will not leave you or forsake you.

Deuteronomy 31:6

Day 14

A BRAVE PERSON IS NOT SOMEONE WHO HAS NO FEAR; IT IS SOMEONE WHO CONQUERS THAT FEAR!

By Terry Cogdell

For years, I struggled with fear. I was afraid of everything — afraid to talk in front of people; afraid to apply for jobs, thinking I wouldn't get hired; I was afraid of getting close to people; afraid of rejection, of being vulnerable. Because I feared betrayal, I put to death the desire to trust others. I was afraid of trying something new because I feared failure. I vowed to never trust again, never be vulnerable again, never attempt anything new again. I put aside all my dreams and hopes.

When I joined my church, Universal Love Peace and Joy, I was new to the ministry, and I saw that my fellow members liked to have everyone participate. When they needed someone to read a scripture or pray or to make announcements, I would avert my eyes or get up and go to the bathroom or just go outside as if I had left something in my car. But when I'd come back in, they would ask me to do something else that I'd be afraid of not doing right.

At one point, I avoided people and crowds. I registered for a program to earn my certification as a life coach. I knew some of my classmates to be very intelligent. I felt intimidated, and when we'd hold a Zoom meeting, I would hide my face and turn off my video. They all spoke of their many degrees and how knowledgeable they were in specific areas. I also had a degree, but I didn't believe I was as knowledgeable as they were. Whenever I'd be called on, I'd say I was gathering my thoughts and would ask that someone else speak. I was afraid of sounding unintelligent. As the course went on, my fears grew worse because sometimes we would have to speak or demonstrate the curriculum in front of the class. I thought I couldn't do it, but I kept trying until I passed my test. While I am a good test taker, I have always found speaking in public a challenge.

I even strategized to avoid public speaking. In Bible school, the teacher asked us students to read aloud or expound on scripture. I asked if I could be last, so by the time the other students finished their lessons, the class was over. The professor said that I would be the first to start the next lesson the following week. My heart pounded so, and because of fear, I didn't show up for the next week's class. Look how fear can rob you of your destiny and dreams!

I learned from my bishop that fear is just false evidence appearing real. I reached a turning point when my church family urged me to push forward, to "do it afraid." They taught me public speaking, and now I can eat fear for breakfast! Whenever

I feel afraid, I just do it anyway, and I let God guide me through. This new perspective helped me with my coaching program, and I am a certified life coach!

To anyone who is reading this: Never let your fears cripple you to the point where you can't reach your goals and dreams. If you're afraid, just do it afraid and trust God to see you through. Just remember that fear is only false evidence appearing real.

Reflect on the fears you struggle with; think back on the thoughts that entered your mind when you first felt fear. Consider the lies that triggered the rippling effects of fear, and remember that it's nothing more than false evidence appearing real.

Let's Pray

Father,

In the name of Jesus, we thank you for those who are reading this story. I pray that they will feel your love for them, and they would remember that you have not given them the spirit of fear, but of love, power and a sound mind.

Thank you, Jesus, that your plans for them are good and not evil, are meant to prosper them and not bring harm, to give them hope and a future. Help them to align their minds to these truths. Bless the reader to overcome all fears and walk in faith. I

In Jesus' name,

Amen

Journal

What is God speaking to you?

About Terry

Terry Cogdell is a woman of faith who loves to praise God. She is an ordained minister, participates in Universal Love, Peace and Joy ministry and is active in her church's outreach programs. Terry is married to Tracy Cogdell. They have three children and two grandchildren. Terry has been an employee of the New York City Police Department's traffic division for 27 years. She is a certified coach and certified timekeeper for the NYC Police Department. She has a bachelor's degree in business administration and has published a book, "Daily Devotional Scriptures Healing Through the Word of God: Mind, Body and Soul." She is working on a collaboration for a children's book and is a co-author of "Live Your Faith Out Loud."

Terry can be reached at: Terrycogdell@gmail.com

EAT FEAR FOR BREAKFAST

Today's Scripture

Peace I leave with you; my peace I give to you, not as the world gives do I give to you. Let not your hearts be troubled, neither let them be afraid.

John 14-27

Day 15

BLEEDING!

By Terry Cogdell

For a year after I had my third child, I had issues with bleeding. I had fibroids and a large cyst. I went to all kinds of doctors and was afraid that I was never going to stop bleeding. They gave me all sorts of medications, but nothing worked; in fact, things got worse. The bleeding got so bad that I had to wear adult diapers, and that didn't contain the bleeding very much. I prayed and asked God, "Why me?" I felt so ashamed thinking that people could see the diaper through my clothes.

There were times when I'd be at work and have to go to the emergency room because I was bleeding so heavily that the blood would leak through my pants.

I had all kinds of tests: EKG, echo test and cat scan. My doctors said I needed a blood transfusion or a hysterectomy, but I never had those surgeries done. The doctors gave me hormone pills to stop the bleeding, but the bleeding didn't stop. I was afraid that I wasn't going live to see my children's children.

Then I had a blessed turning point. I was at a visiting church function, and the pastor said, "Today, someone is going be healed." The power of God hit me so hard that I began to run around the church. I was healed! I no longer bled, and I no longer feared I wouldn't live to see my grandchildren. I thank God for his healing power that fell upon me. I am a walking miracle, and I share my testimony everywhere I go, telling of the mercy and grace of God.

Fear is something we all experience, but if we can realize that fear's agenda is to stop the plans and purpose God has for your life, then we can know that God also has an agenda for us. We know this from the words of Jeremiah 29-11: For I know the plans I have for you, declares the Lord, plans for welfare and not for evil, to give you a future and a hope.

Let's Pray

Jesus,

I thank you that you are for me and not against me. I thank you that freedom is found in you. I invite you today into every fearful thought, and I pray that you shine a light exposing the lie whilst declaring your truth over my life. I am so grateful that I don't have to walk this life journey alone. Thank you for never leaving me nor forsaking me.

Amen

Journal

What is God speaking to you?

EAT FEAR FOR BREAKFAST

About Terry

Terry Cogdell is a woman of faith who loves to praise God. She is an ordained minister, participates in Universal Love, Peace and Joy ministry and is active in her church's outreach programs. Terry is married to Tracy Cogdell. They have three children and two grandchildren. Terry has been an employee of the New York City Police Department's traffic division for 27 years. She is a certified coach and certified timekeeper for the NYC Police Department. She has a bachelor's *degree in business administration and has published a book, "Daily Devotional Scriptures Healing Through the Word of God: Mind, Body and Soul." She is working on a collaboration for a children's book and is a co-author of "Live Your Faith Out Loud."*

Terry can be reached at: Terrycogdell@gmail.com

EAT FEAR FOR BREAKFAST

Today's Scripture

Beloved, I pray that all may go well with you and that you may be in good health, as it goes well with your soul.

3 John 1:2

Day 16

BINGE EATING FEAR FOR BREAKFAST

By T.L. Blythers

There is nothing more excruciating than knowing you have failed. One of my greatest failures turned out to be an impactful, life-changing experience. At the time, I thought my life plan was done! Haphazardly, I had invested three to four years at a university, and my attitude along with a shameful GPA had hit rock bottom. While attempting to clean up this educational debacle, I found myself standing in the middle of a junior college chorus classroom desperate for a scholarship. The choir director nonchalantly requested a song. Here? Right now? Just sing? Immediately, fear launched an unexpected attack. But to God be the glory, within an instant, my spirit activated my faith, and I refused to accept defeat. Confidently, I reached deep down into my musical reservoir and bellowed out a perfectly pitched, melodious and emotional acapella rendition of "The National Anthem." I seized that moment and appreciated the monumental magnitude of being given an opportunity. Three things will give you a life advantage, and they're the perfect elixir for success:

- Vision
- Preparation
- Hope

Learn how to correctly differentiate a "window of opportunity" and "door of opportunity." There's a distinct draft and airflow that shifts the atmosphere when a door, as opposed to a window, is opened. The way an opportunity is perceived is a direct correlation to the intensity level of pursuit. I'm reminded of how Jacob wrestled with an angel in the Bible. When the angel demanded Jacob to let him go, Jacob replied, "I'm not going to let you go until you bless my soul!" When you become that relentless, that's when you've dined at the table of faith and devoured fear. By the way, I received a choir scholarship that day, and it changed the trajectory of my life. Be encouraged. 3 John 1:2: "Beloved, I wish above all things that thou mayest prosper and be in health, even as thy soul prospereth."

Let's Pray

Father God,

Increase our faith and bind the oppressive spirits of worry, doubt and anxiety. Fill us with hope and vision. Download your plans, peace and preparation into our hearts. Thank you for your strong arm of direction.

Amen!

Journal

What is God speaking to you?

About Tamika

Tamika L. Blythers is a master trainer and facilitator, author, educator, entrepreneur, consultant and transformational speaker. Her platform, "V.O.W" 9 points of Impact, is a simple shared message of self-inquiry, which requires individuals to radically change perspectives about decisions and goals in life. Her consulting business, EduVizon, LLC, provides empowerment education and hosting/emcee services designed to enhance, energize, transform and achieve premium results. She has authored numerous books, and several are best sellers. She is the "Upperroom Writer." T.L. Blythers stands firmly on the life principle, "You are a product of your expectations, not the limitations."

Email: tblythers@gmail.com
Social Media: FB/tlblythersauthor

EAT FEAR FOR BREAKFAST

Today's Scripture

You prepare a table before me in the presence of my enemies.

Psalm 23:5

Day 17

5-STAR DINING, MAIN COURSE: FEAR

By T.L. Blythers

There is nothing more intimidating than a formal dinner table setting. All the silverware, four glasses, plates, chargers, napkins…do you start with this one to the left or is it the right side? One thing is for sure: Fear will be an uninvited guest.

I have found myself at many tables by way of invitation or through strategic preparation. It was quite terrifying. Nevertheless, I chose to shift fear's seat and assignment. When I changed my mindset and increased my faith, fear had a new meaning. The next time you prepare to dine at God's divine table, walk in the room confidently; take your seat at the table and feast on this 5-star spread!

Star 1: Faith eradicates fright (you deserve it and belong there)

Star 2: Foundation not frustration (stand firm on your beliefs)
Star 3: Expectation, never exemption (don't count yourself out)
Star 4: Anticipation strikes out anxiety (stop overthinking)
Star 5: Revelation defeats rejection (you are enough)

Let's Pray

Father God,

Thank you for a renewed mindset, heart and spirit. You are our sustainer and supporter, protector and provider, and the lifter of our heads. Through you, we are victorious!

Amen!

EAT FEAR FOR BREAKFAST
Journal

What is God speaking to you?

About Tamika

Tamika L. Blythers is a master trainer and facilitator, author, educator, entrepreneur, consultant and transformational speaker. Her platform, "V.O.W" 9 points of Impact, is a simple shared message of self-inquiry, which requires individuals to radically change perspectives about decisions and goals in life. Her consulting business, EduVizon, LLC, provides empowerment education and hosting/emcee services designed to enhance, energize, transform and achieve *premium results. She has authored numerous books, and several are best sellers. She is the "Upperroom Writer." T.L. Blythers stands firmly on the life principle, "You are a product of your expectations, not the limitations."*

Email: tblythers@gmail.com
Social Media: FB/tlblythersauthor

EAT FEAR FOR BREAKFAST

Today's Scripture

*He who dwells in the shelter of the Most High will abide in the shadow of the Almighty.
I will say to the Lord, "My refuge and my fortress, my God, in whom I trust."*

Psalm 9:1-2

Day 18

BREAKING FREE: FINDING STRENGTH IN GOD'S SHELTER

By Dr. Valarie W. Harris

There was a time in my life when I struggled deeply with fear, especially when battling alcoholism and obesity for years. The fear stemmed from losing my father to cirrhosis of the liver, which cast a long shadow over my life. Alcoholism became a formidable adversary, and obesity bound me with various health challenges.

Amid this struggle, I sought help and embraced the power of counseling. There is nothing wrong with sitting in the counselor's chair to combat the challenges we face in life. This journey was not easy, but it was necessary. Along the way, I found solace and reassurance as God spoke to me through Psalm 91:1-2: "He who dwells in the shelter of the Most High will abide in the shadow of the Almighty. I will say to the Lord, 'My refuge and my fortress, my God, in whom I trust.'" These verses reminded me that God is my refuge and fortress, a constant source of strength and protection.

Through faith and the support of counseling, I began to overcome these challenges. The reassurance from God's Word gave me the courage to confront my fears and transform my life. Today, I have broken free from alcoholism and obesity. Instead, I stand as a testament to the power of faith and the importance of seeking help when needed.

By sharing my story, I hope to inspire others facing similar struggles to seek support and strength in God's promises. Together, we can overcome our fears and embrace a life of health and empowerment.

Let's Pray

Heavenly Father,

Thank you for your unwavering love and guidance. As we reflect on our struggles and triumphs, we are reminded of your promise in Psalm 91:1-2, that those who dwell in your shelter will find refuge and strength in your shadow.

Lord, we ask for your grace to fill our hearts and minds, giving us the courage to seek help and the wisdom to embrace the support around us. Remind us that there is no shame in asking for assistance, for it is through our humility that your strength is made perfect.

May we always remember that you are our refuge and fortress, a constant source of protection and encouragement. Help us to trust in your promises and to lean on you in times of need, knowing that you will guide us through every trial.

Inspire us to break free from the chains that hold us back, to overcome our fears, and to walk boldly in the path you have set before us. Let our lives be a testament to your redeeming power and unwavering support.

We pray that each reader finds hope and strength in these words, drawing closer to you and finding peace in your presence.

In Jesus' name,

Amen

Journal

What is God speaking to you?

About Dr. Valarie

Dr. Valarie W. Harris is a prominent figure in education, leadership and personal development, boasting over four decades of dedicated service. As a certified empowerment coach and business consultant, Dr. Valarie has profoundly impacted educators, women leaders and aspiring entrepreneurs, fostering a legacy of empowerment and success.

Dr. Valarie's academic journey is a testament to an unwavering commitment to excellence. Holding a bachelor's degree from Norfolk State University and a master's degree from Virginia Tech University, Dr. Valarie has further enriched her education with degrees from Seraphim Ministries International Bible College and Liberty University, culminating in a doctoral degree.

Beyond academic achievements, Dr. Valarie has a global perspective, highlighted by involvement in missions to Ghana and disaster relief efforts in Grenada. These experiences underscore a dedication to humanitarian causes and uplifting underserved communities.

As the founder of "Stepping Out with Purpose," Dr. Valarie inspires others to unlock their hidden potential and achieve their life's purpose. Dr. Valarie's teaching and writing style blends motivation, guidance, and actionable advice, significantly impacting readers and audiences alike.

With a passion for empowering others, Dr. Valarie continues to lead transformative journeys, helping individuals embrace growth, overcome fears, and achieve their dreams.

steppingout@talktimeval.com

https://www.facebook.com/valarie.harris.716/

EAT FEAR FOR BREAKFAST

Today's Scripture

*So do not fear not, for I am with you;
be not dismayed, for I am your God;
I will strengthen you, I will help you,
I will uphold you with my righteous right hand.*

Isaiah 41:10

EAT FEAR FOR BREAKFAST

Day 19

FROM REJECTION TO REDEMPTION: OVERCOMING FEAR WITH FAITH

By Dr. Valarie W. Harris

As a child and young adult, I struggled deeply with the fear of rejection and ridicule. The sting of rejection hit hard when I discovered the identity of one of my grandfathers. He did not take kindly to this revelation, leaving me feeling unwanted and dismissed. Another painful incident occurred in the classroom when a teacher called me a moron in front of the entire class. The humiliation was so intense that it paralyzed me, making me hesitant to move forward and always finding excuses for why I couldn't meet expectations. This rejection held me captive well into adulthood.

During my despair, God spoke to me through Isaiah 41:10:

"So do not fear, for I am with you; do not be dismayed, for I am your God. I will strengthen you and help you; I will uphold you with my righteous right hand." These words became a lifeline, reminding me that I was never alone and that God was always with me, ready to strengthen and support me.

Embracing this scripture, I began to feel a profound sense of deliverance. God's promise of unwavering support pushed me past my debilitating fear and rejection. I realized that with God by my side, I had the strength to rise above the hurtful experiences of my past.

Today, I praise God for this deliverance. I have transformed my pain into a source of empowerment, enabling me to help others overcome similar fears in their lives.

By sharing my story and the strength I found in God's promise, I guide others towards the same divine courage that helped me break free. Through faith, I have moved from rejection to redemption, and now I dedicate myself to empowering others to do the same.

Let's Pray

Heavenly Father,

Thank you for your unwavering love, support and strength. When I faced rejection and ridicule, you spoke to me through Isaiah 41:10, reminding me not to fear, for you are with me. Your promise gave me the courage to rise above my fears.

Lord, I pray for those struggling with fear and rejection. Fill them with your strength and remind them that you are always by their side. Help them to find hope and deliverance in your promises.

Use my story to encourage and uplift others, guiding them to overcome their fears and embrace your love and support.

In Jesus' name,

Amen

Journal

What is God speaking to you?

About Dr. Valarie

Dr. Valarie W. Harris is a prominent figure in education, leadership and personal development, boasting over four decades of dedicated service. As a certified empowerment coach and business consultant, Dr. Valarie has profoundly impacted educators, women leaders and aspiring entrepreneurs, fostering a legacy of empowerment and success.

Dr. Valarie's academic journey is a testament to an unwavering commitment to excellence. Holding a bachelor's degree from Norfolk State University and a master's degree from Virginia Tech University, Dr. Valarie has further enriched her education with degrees from Seraphim Ministries International Bible College and Liberty University, culminating in a doctoral degree.

Beyond academic achievements, Dr. Valarie has a global perspective, highlighted by involvement in missions to Ghana and disaster relief efforts in Grenada. These experiences underscore a dedication to humanitarian causes and uplifting underserved communities.

As the founder of "Stepping Out with Purpose," Dr. Valarie inspires others to unlock their hidden potential and achieve their life's purpose. Dr. Valarie's teaching and writing style blends motivation, guidance, and actionable advice, significantly impacting readers and audiences alike.

With a passion for empowering others, Dr. Valarie continues to lead transformative journeys, helping individuals embrace growth, overcome fears, and achieve their dreams.

steppingout@talktimeval.com

https://www.facebook.com/valarie.harris.716/

EAT FEAR FOR BREAKFAST

Today's Scripture

Teach me your way, O Lord, that I may walk in your truth; unite my heart to fear your name.

Psalm 86:11

Day 20

THERE IS A TIME FOR EVERYTHING

By Adiesa Monique

Have you ever been in a situation where you were afraid of someone? Has your life or safety been threatened by another human being? There was a time in my life where I was in a relationship that was controlled on every level. I believed what this person said to me because this type of fear was different. They had an extremely violent nature and would constantly try to provoke me. The constant yelling, lying and threats were almost unbearable. It got to a point where I wanted to defend myself and get rid of the threat.

I started to realize that I did not want to be afraid, and I had to stand up for myself. I knew that I was not supposed to be fearful of anyone except God. One of the scriptures that brought this to my attention is Proverbs 29:25 ESV: The fear of man lays a snare, but whoever trusts in the Lord is safe. This opened my eyes to the real enemy, and I decided to deal with this head on. This situation showed me where I was at fault. I know God wasn't mad at me, but what was happening was what I had allowed to happen. I realized that violence had a propensity to distort my thinking, and it was not okay. Fear in this circumstance altered my thinking into a warped reality. I dealt with this plight in the spiritual and natural, and I had to leave.

    My healing began when I repented to God for the part I played in this situation. I had to realize that God's Word takes precedence in my life, no matter what the problem is or whoever is in the equation. I had to remove myself and believe God at his Word to line up with his will for my life. I am truly glad that God intervened in my life, and I am a changed woman.

Let's Pray

Dear Heavenly Father,

I am grateful that there is no problem in my life that is too difficult for you. Thank you for your immeasurable mercy and extended grace in my life. Keep me wrapped in your arms and in the palm of your right hand. Thank you for being a shepherd that will leave the 99 and come after the one.

Amen

Journal

What is God speaking to you?

About Adiesa

Adiesa Monique is a retired U.S. Army combat veteran with associate degrees of applied science in human services and medical assistance. She has a passion for assisting others along their healing path from trauma and abuse. She uses her experience and witty personality that saved her from destruction to help other women navigate their own healing journey. She has been graced to have 22 years and counting of sobriety and uses her knowledge to mentor others. She is an advocate for individuals struggling with addictions, which is her true calling. She also uses her military experiences to help foster and implement strategies for successful outcomes in different scenarios. She attributes her willingness to help others overcome obstacles to God and her support system. She continues to pursue her aspirations for excellence in every area of her life.

You may connect with Adiesa at Adiesamonique.com and Adiesa Monique Facebook page.

EAT FEAR FOR BREAKFAST

Today's Scripture

*For I am the Lord, your God,
who takes hold of your right hand
and says to you, "Do not fear; I will help
you."*

Isaiah 41:13

Day 21

PUT YOUR DOG ON A LEASH

By Adiesa Monique

There was a time in my life when I did not like dogs. I did everything possible to stay as far away from them. The fear I had would be so crippling that I would either freeze or scream to the top of my lungs if a dog approached me.

I got tired of my reactions to dogs and needed a solution. I wanted to know how I got to this point in my life. I'd grown up with cats and dogs in my home. I could not pinpoint the root of my fear. I reflected on my childhood and remembered an incident that happened when I was around 8 years old. I was in my bedroom, jumping on the bed, and I vividly recall one of my brothers opening the door and throwing a stray cat in my room, ,then immediately shutting the door.

The cat was trying to attack me. I was screaming, and nobody came to my rescue. I was finally able to jump from my bed over the cat and get out of my room. That scenario caused a lot of trauma and anxiety for me.

    In 2021, I met a neighbor, and she had a huge dog she would walk all the time. I eventually befriended her and told her I needed to get over my fear of dogs, and I asked her if I could walk with her and her dog. She thought it was an excellent idea, and she obliged. There were mornings that I would get up, and we would walk around our neighborhood and eventually go to the beach. That was a huge turning point for me. I started to face the fear because I was exhausted from being fearful. I often wondered why my experience with a cat made me afraid of dogs, but today, I'm grateful that I'm not afraid of either.

Let's Pray

Dear God,

   According to your Word In Psalm 34:4 ESV: I sought the Lord, and he answered me and delivered me from all my fears.
   I thank you that for my fears and anxiety, you will give me peace.

Amen

EAT FEAR FOR BREAKFAST

Journal

What is God speaking to you?

_____
_____
_____
_____
_____
_____
_____
_____
_____
_____
_____
_____
_____
_____
_____
_____
_____
_____
_____
_____
_____

About Adiesa

Adicsa Monique is a retired U.S. Army combat veteran with associate degrees of applied science in human services and medical assistance. She has a passion for assisting others along their healing path from trauma and abuse. She uses her experience and witty personality that saved her from destruction to help other women navigate their own healing journey. She has been graced to have 22 years and counting of sobriety and uses her knowledge to mentor others. She is an advocate for individuals struggling with addictions, which is her true calling. She also uses her military experiences to help foster and implement strategies for successful outcomes in different scenarios. She attributes her willingness to help others overcome obstacles to God and her support system. She continues to pursue her aspirations for excellence in every area of her life.

You may connect with Adiesa at Adiesamonique.com and Adiesa Monique Facebook page.

EAT FEAR FOR BREAKFAST

Today's Scripture

Behold, I will bring to it health and healing, and I will heal them and reveal to them abundance of prosperity and security.

Jeremiah 33:6

Day 22

FEARLESS RESILIENCE: FINDING DIVINE HEALING AND EXCEEDING ABUNDANCE IN TRIALS

By Amber Krystal

Now to him who is able to do far more abundantly than all that we ask or think, according to the power at work within us, to him be glory in the church by Christ Jesus throughout all ages, world without end, Amen. (Ephesians 3:20-21)

Life often presents us with challenges that can feel overwhelming, pushing us to the brink of despair in fear. However, it is during these times of suffering, trials and tribulation, that we are given the opportunity to grow, renew and restore ourselves through God's immense power and love.

Ephesians 3: 20-21 reminds us of the boundless power of God, who is able to do immeasurably more than we could ever ask or imagine. His power is at work within us, bringing glory to him through our lives. Jeremiah 33:6 assures us of God's promise to bring health and healing, allowing us to experience abundant peace and security.

I have faced my own share of trials and tribulations. There was a time when I was overwhelmed with fear, feeling utterly betrayed and lost. My journey included facing an indictment, going through a painful divorce and experiencing profound, personal betrayal. Each of these experiences seemed designed to break me to push me into the abyss of fear and failure.

Yet, it was precisely in these moments of deepest darkness that I found the most profound light. Through my suffering, I was reintroduced to God in a way that was powerful and divine. He became a source of strength and restoration. As I navigated through these tumultuous waters, I learned to let go of fear and to embrace the suffering as a means to grow stronger and more resilient. God's promise in Jeremiah 33:6 came alive in my life, as he began to heal my wounds, both seen and unseen. I found health and healing, not only physically, but also emotionally and spiritually.

His peace became my anchor, and his power enabled me to overcome the fear that once paralyzed me. I encourage you see your trials not as setbacks, but as set-ups for a greater come back. Let your suffering and tribulations be the refining fire that purifies and strengthens you. Embrace your journey, knowing that God is with you every step of the way, ready to bring you health, healing and abundant peace. Do not allow fear to control you or to dictate the course of your life.

Instead, let God's immeasurable power work within you, renewing your spirit and restoring your hope. Trust in his promises and let his glory shine through your resilience and triumph.

Let's Pray

Heavenly Father,

We thank you for your boundless power in your promise of healing and peace. Help us to overcome our fears and trust in your divine plan for our lives. May we embrace our trials and tribulations, knowing that they are opportunities for growth and renewal. Strengthen us, Lord, and let your glory be revealed in our lives, as we try over adversity. In Jesus' name, we pray. Amen.

Remember, count it as all joy when you face trials and tribulations. Know that God does his best work during those times. He is waiting to do more than you can ever imagine. Embrace his healing and let his peace guard your hearts as you walk in fearless resilience.

Amen

Journal

What is God speaking to you?

About Amber

Amber Krystal is the founder of Be Healed, Be Whole, Be Mature Ministries - A Place of Metamorphosis. Anointed to heal the brokenhearted, Amber is called to empower, inspire and motivate individuals to emerge into their true selves. Having endured profound suffering, Amber faced a private divorce from a pastor she was married to for 14 years. Her ex-husband's hidden life led to a federal indictment, imprisonment and a heart-wrenching divorce, almost pushing her into the *shadows despair. Yet, her journey from pain to healing serves as a beacon of hope, inspiring others to embark on their own path of healing and self-discovery. Amber's unique approach helps women uncover their true potential, offering relatable authenticity and hope to women from all walks of life. Amber is a speaker, teacher and thought leader.*

Email: contact@hwmministries.com

Today's Scripture

... and forgive us our debts, as we also have forgiven our debtors.

Matthew 6:12

Day 23

AFTER I DON'T ...

By Carla Fitzgerald

One of the happiest moments in my life was the day I said, "I do", to the man who'd won my heart. When I uttered those words before God, family and friends, I meant them for life. I never fathomed that my "I do" would eventually become, "I don't ... anymore!"

Infidelity had interrupted the sanctity of my marriage, and slowly and painfully, it began crumbling at the seam. How could the person I'd given all of who I am have betrayed my trust and shattered the covenant we declared? This level of betrayal was incomprehensible.

Journeying through divorce was like a nightmare that wouldn't end — a funeral for someone I once loved. I wasn't equipped to navigate through that kind of pain or the stigma of shame that accompanied it. Divorce was not supposed to happen to me, or so I believed, as if I were exempt from the tricks of the enemy. And that's the takeaway from this message.

While it would be easy to focus on the infidelity, that's not the purpose here. The point is to recognize and understand Satan's age-old antics —– to kill, steal and destroy anything God has declared "good." That's his sole purpose. But a coin has two sides, and here's where Satan failed. He didn't factor in the power of God in my life, and that was a huge mistake!

Through the hurt and shame, a good friend supported and taught me how to trust God through the process, which eventually, led to me forgiving my now ex-husband. You see, if I had never forgiven him, the enemy would have not only destroyed my marriage but also would have sequestered the power and authority God has given me over him.

If Jesus has forgiven me of all of my sins against him, it would be an injustice to not forgive my ex for his sins against me. Forgiveness is not just the right thing to do, according to the opening passage; it's a requirement. After all, God loves him just as much as he loves me. So, if you haven't forgiven someone who's hurt you, right now is a good time to do so.

Let's Pray

Heavenly Father,

Thank you for forgiving me of all of my sins. And thank you for giving me power and authority over all the power of the enemy. Therefore, I am confident that nothing will, by any means, hurt me. Finally, Father, I forgive others, just as you have forgiven me.

In Jesus' name,

Amen

Journal

What is God speaking to you?

About Carla

Carla Fitzgerald is passionate about helping others see themselves through the lens of God and experience healing from the soul outward. Encouraged by a friend during her own personal and spiritual journey, Carla now pays that encouragement forward through Pit to Palace Ministries' Empowerment Workshops (Augusta, Ga.) and other related events/venues. Carla is also co-author of the Amazon Best Seller book, "Live Your Faith Out Loud, Volume 3."

Carla can be reached at BreakthroughCreationsInc@gmail.com.

EAT FEAR FOR BREAKFAST

Today's Scripture

A voice cries in the wilderness, prepare the way of the Lord; make straight in the desert a highway for our God.

Isaiah 40:3

Day 24

WHEN BEING YOURSELF DOESN'T SEEM TO BE ENOUGH

By Carla Fitzgerald

Have you ever felt like you were out of place? That you didn't fit in or measure up to those in your circle? That you were unexplainably different? Well, that's my story.

For years I struggled with wanting to fit in with the crowd. From my perspective, just being myself didn't seem to be enough, and a façade of being someone I wasn't enslaved me into a constant mode of pretense. Sadly, I practiced that unscripted role playing for so long that I lost my identity. The truth of the matter is that I was a home-grown, country girl from rural Mississippi, desperately desiring to fit in. I was ashamed of being who God had created me to be.

Eventually, I grew tired of the pretense, even stopped playing church and deepened my relationship with God. Reading my Bible and listening to biblical teachings helped me realize I was already enough and had been "enough" from the day I was born. Prior to learning the Word of God, I was blinded by a lack of knowledge and self-worth. I didn't know that I was already fearfully and wonderfully made or that I had been made in God's image. That's why I couldn't fit in with the crowd. The purpose was calling, but I wasn't listening or answering.

In fact, in 2019, when God spoke these words to me: "Prepare ye the way of the Lord," I didn't understand why he would give me that scripture in the tune of a song.

I asked God, "What does that mean? And, since I don't write music, why give me those words in a song?" However, the melody was so clear that I recorded it.

Propelling forward, recently I was asked to conduct a Bible study teaching from Matthew, chapter 3. I opened the chapter and read the heading: "Prepare Ye the Way of the Lord." I gasped! I finally understood why I'd been given that scripture in 2019. God was instructing me to become a "voice crying out," telling others about his coming. Well, that's exactly what I am in the process of doing, and fear will not stop my calling and purpose! Don't let it stop yours, either!

Let's Pray

Father God,

Thank you for allowing me to be the voice crying out to those who do not know you. Understanding that I am enough, I thank you for handpicking me to help save souls and build lives for your kingdom. I honor being fearfully and wonderfully made in your image, and I "eat fear for breakfast" as I boldly declare your word.

In Jesus; name,

Amen

Journal

What is God speaking to you?

About Carla

Carla Fitzgerald is passionate about helping others see themselves through the lens of God and experience healing from the soul outward. Encouraged by a friend during her own personal and spiritual journey, Carla now pays that encouragement forward through Pit to Palace Ministries' Empowerment Workshops (Augusta, Ga.) and other related events/venues. Carla is also co-author of the Amazon Best Seller book, "Live Your Faith Out Loud, Volume 3."

Carla can be reached at BreakthroughCreationsInc@gmail.com.

EAT FEAR FOR BREAKFAST

Today's Scripture

And the peace of God, which surpasses all understanding, will guard your hearts and your minds in Christ Jesus.

Philippians 4:7

EAT FEAR FOR BREAKFAST

Day 25

PERSONAL ENCOUNTER

By Ethel Lewis-Polite

According to the latest data released by the National Crime Records Bureau, a staggering 22,372 housewives tragically took their own lives in the past year. This equates to an average of 61 suicides every day or one every 25 minutes.

After dropping off my kids at school, I returned home and decided to take a moment for myself. I brewed a cup of tea and settled onto the couch, reflecting on everything that had been happening in my life. It felt like everything was falling apart — my husband had betrayed me by having an affair and had drained my bank account with fraudulent checks, taking everything I had. I was so overwhelmed with emotions, I couldn't help but break down in a flood of tears, seeking God in prayer and trying to figure out how I was going to move forward.

At that very moment, I questioned my own worthiness of love. Having already gone through one failed marriage, now I was facing another one. Why wasn't I deserving of someone's love? My husbands enjoyed being taken care of by me but didn't reciprocate the same love that I had for them. It felt like I was valued only for my ability to care for others and was not truly loved in return. The idea of taking a handful of pills to end the fear and pain within me crossed my mind. My tears flowed uncontrollably, and exhaustion eventually overcame me, leading me into a deep sleep.

When I awoke, I felt an indescribable peace that surpassed all understanding. Even though my circumstances hadn't changed, deep down I knew that God was assuring me that everything would be all right. In that peaceful slumber, I had a profound encounter with God, and he granted me relief from my worries. I discovered my purpose for living — my children. If I had succumbed to thoughts of suicide, I would have missed out on seeing their incredible successes and fulfilling the divine calling that God had not placed on not only my life, but also on the lives of my children.

John 10:10 says, "The thief only comes to steal and kill and destroy. I came (Jesus) that they may have life and have it abundantly. Always remember, God has a plan for your life."

Let's Pray

Thank you, Lord,

For your loving kindness and tender mercies towards me. Thank you for rescuing me and healing me when you saw that my strength was gone. I will always give thanks to you Lord, for you are good, and your steadfast love endures forever. I give you thanks in all my circumstances; for this is the will of God in Christ Jesus for me.

Amen

EAT FEAR FOR BREAKFAST

Journal

What is God speaking to you?

About Ethel

Ethel Lewis-Polito is dedicated to accompanying women on their journey to conquer their fears and fulfill their divine purpose. She is honored to hold the esteemed positions of a licensed minister and a certified Christian life coach. Ethel has earned an Associate of Arts degree in Biblical Studies from Southwest Bible College & Seminary and has taken the initiative to establish a women's ministry, Joy In Hope Ministries Inc.

EAT FEAR FOR BREAKFAST

These accomplishments stand as a testament to the profound impact of faith and the unwavering guidance of the Lord.

Ethel may be reached at ethelpolite24@gmail.com and www.joyinhopeministries.com.

EAT FEAR FOR BREAKFAST

EAT FEAR FOR BREAKFAST

Today's Scripture

When I am afraid, I put my trust in you.

Psalm 56:3-4

Day 26

NEVER LET FEAR STOP YOU, FOR GOD IS WITH YOU

By Dr. Bronwyn M. Davis

As I prepare to share my story, I am reminded of several things related to experiencing fear. Being someone who has always wanted to play it safe and do things that I am comfortable with, I struggled when opportunities came that stretched me and took me out of my comfort zone. I enjoy speaking and teaching. At my former church, I had become comfortable with being a Sunday School teacher and was fine with that. I was excited to be growing in God's Word and teaching our small class in the basement, or lower level, I should say, of our church.

Well, I was presented with an opportunity to be a women's conference session speaker. With this opportunity, there was no option to back out. I was so nervous because this was my first ministry speaking engagement at a sister church. When I reviewed the speaker lineup, I really began to shake. My only outlet at that point would have been for my job to decline my time off, but my time off was granted. I could see that nothing was working to get me out of this speaking opportunity.

Not only was I nervous, I also needed to confirm the scripture I was to be speaking on. I had been apprised of the conference theme, but not my scripture. God is so amazing, though. The conference organizer, the church's First Lady, and I kept missing each other's phone calls. But God in his faithfulness towards us gave me the scripture, Jeremiah 50, during my prayer time in seeking him. It was after God gave me the scripture that the First Lady and I connected, and she confirmed that the scripture I'd received was the one!

The session I presented was amazing, and the class was packed wall to wall! I even remember losing my place in my notes a few times, but God was there. This was the push I needed to come up out of the basement. For those who want to play it small or play it safe, I want to remind you that we serve a big God, so come up out of the basement; take your place in the front of the line!

Let's Pray

God,

I thank you that I no longer play small because you are a big God! Your Word says that you will never leave me nor forsake me. You have not given us the spirit of fear, but of power, and love, and of a sound mind. You will personally go before me, neither failing nor abandoning me. So, Lord, I thank you for walking with me, leading and guiding me. Lord, I place my trust in you to move beyond fear for you are with me.

Amen

Journal

What is God speaking to you?

About Dr. Bronwyn

Dr. Bronwyn M. Davis is a master's-prepared licensed professional counselor (LPC), certified coach, speaker, instructor, mentor, contributing author ("God's Compassion Towards Me" and "Celebrating 365 Days of Gratitude") and a licensed minister of the gospel.

In ministry, Bronwyn has served for over 25 years in many capacities. Bronwyn obtained a doctorate in religious education from Destiny School of Ministry (DSM) in 2020 and teaches at DSM for the Christian

Counseling Institute. Bronwyn is the founder and executive director of A Safe Place Clinical Counseling, PLLC in Michigan. Bronwyn is a member of Evangel Christian Church in Roseville, Michigan. As a counselor, Bronwyn possesses a genuine interest in others, an ability to listen and a sincere desire to see others healed, empowered and succeeding in life.

Bronwyn may be reached at BronwynMD@yahoo.com.

EAT FEAR FOR BREAKFAST

Today's Scripture

*For if you keep silent at this time; relief and deliverance will rise for the Jews from another place, but you and your father's house will perish.
And who knows whether you have come to the kingdom for such a time as this?*

Esther 4:14

Day 27

EMBRACE FAITH: FLOURISH WITHOUT FEAR

By Dr. Sanja Rickette Stinson

Stepping forward into the role of nonprofit founding CEO wasn't easy. Even though I come from parents who were entrepreneurs who taught each of their children that entrepreneurship was the way to build a legacy for generations to come, taking on the role was still scary and brought a lot of fear. There weren't many black women in my role, and there was no support.

This is why I am so grateful to my parents. Despite witnessing the burning of their business during the 1968 riots, suffering setbacks, struggling because of discrimination, being overlooked, and fearing closure, they never allowed fear to stop them. They remained faithful, kept themselves encouraged, acted, and resolved to continue building their legacy for their children and future generations.

EAT FEAR FOR BREAKFAST

The story of Esther is deeply personal for me when I think about "Eating Fear for Breakfast." It not only tells a powerful story of a woman stepping into a crucial leadership role but also reveals how fear can paralyze us, hindering us from walking in our God-designed purpose.

When I read the entire story of Esther, I see how others can make us believe that we are not worthy of the honor of stepping forward to lead, especially in roles such as pastoral leadership, nonprofit leadership, business leadership, or transformational leadership. This is often because of gender bias that surfaces in various denominations and business ventures and persists even in the 21st century. It feels as if a woman's capacity to lead is diminished or devalued simply because of her gender. I was recently reminded that the story of Esther teaches us invaluable lessons about "eating fear for breakfast".

Faithfulness: Esther's story is a testament to overcoming societal barriers and embracing the call to leadership with faith, courage, and resilience. It teaches us that faithfulness is the first step to overcoming fear. Despite everything, Esther had to remain faithful to God's plan and timing. She had to trust God in her purpose and not allow fear to control her, her destiny, or the destiny of the people she was called to serve.

Encouragement: It is clear that Esther faced an incredibly dangerous situation that could have cost her life. Yet, she had to find encouragement and encourage herself, believing that God had already equipped her for the task she was called to. Leaders, especially black women, can get discouraged at times. However, knowing that God has equipped us and made provisions ahead of us allows us to be encouraged, trusting that God is with us every step of the way.

Action: Deciding to act was no easy task for Esther because there were real fears and threats. Considering that the law prohibited approaching the king unless summoned and weighing the potential consequences of being turned away by the king, one can understand that the danger was very real. Nevertheless, Esther had to trust that God was with her and believe that he would uphold her as she approached the king. "Do it scared; do it afraid" is the first step to learning to "eat fear for breakfast." It involves acting with the confidence that God has you, despite any perceived inadequacies. God is able to sustain and support us, but we must act and trust him, even when we can't see his hand at work.

Resolve: Resolve means having a firm determination to do something or to continue on a course of action, despite any difficulties or obstacles. Esther's journey was fraught with risk and potential failure, but she resolved to step forward and face the challenges head-on. She leaned into God's strength, relying less on her own. With firm determination, Esther acted to save her people. Today, as women and kingdom believers, we, too, must resolve to be determined to transform the lives of others through our courage and perseverance, despite the various obstacles we face, because God has already provided the way forward.

The book of Esther serves as a powerful reminder that we never face fear alone. God will carry us through every situation. Just as Esther rose to her calling, we, too, are called to rise for such a time as this. Let's go, eat fear for breakfast and rise to our calling. God has given you the equipment and knowledge to step into your purpose and destiny. For such a time as this, let us step forward into our purpose and destiny.

Let's Pray

Heavenly Father,

Thank you for the powerful reminder from the book of Esther that we are never alone in facing our fears. Help us to rise to our calling with faith and courage, just as Esther did. Strengthen us to step forward into our purpose and destiny, knowing that you are with us every step of the way. Empower us to face each challenge with confidence, trusting in your provision and guidance.

In Jesus' name, we pray,

Amen

Journal

What is God speaking to you?

About Dr. Sanja

Recognized as a thought leader, Dr. Sanja Rickette Stinson brings over four decades of invaluable experience as the founding CEO of Matthew House - Chicago, a supportive service center for the homeless. Raised by entrepreneurial parents, Gus and Mary Rickette, Dr. Sanja carries forward a legacy of leadership and innovation.

Dr. Sanja is the president of Empower Her Ventures, LLC, and founder of Dr. Sanja Coaching & Consulting, where she is dedicated to transforming the lives of faith-based and professional women over the age of 50. Her mission is to empower these women to embrace their roles as disruptors, encouraging them to reframe and reimagine their lives with a focus on self-care and rejuvenation.

Beyond her nonprofit leadership, Dr. Sanja is a certified coach, business strategist, speaker, best-selling author, blogger and ordained minister. Through these channels, she inspires individuals to unlock their leadership potential and pursue personal growth. Her best-selling anthology trilogy collection, "Disrupting the Status Quo," underscores her commitment to visionary leadership, ministry and community development. This dedication has amplified her impact globally, making her a sought-after speaker at international conferences and events. She has also co-authored works such as "Trailblazers 2," "Possibilities Unlimited," and "Dare to Rise Above Mediocrity" alongside renowned figures like Les Brown and Dr. Cheryl Wood.

Dr. Sanja served as the founding pastor of Victory & Grace Christian Church and was commissioned as an apostle in 2018. She has ordained ministers and currently serves as the pastor emeritus of Victory & Grace Christian Church. Her academic journey includes degrees from DePaul University, McCormick Theological Seminary, Concordia University and Northern Theological Seminary. Dr. Sanja's relentless pursuit of excellence shows no signs of abating.

For those seeking to connect with her, inquiries can be directed to:

Website: drsanja.com

EAT FEAR FOR BREAKFAST

Today's Scripture

... for God gave us a spirit not of fear but of power and love and self-control.

2 Timothy 1:7

Day 28

CONQUERING THE FEAR FACTOR

By Dr. Stacy L. Henderson

The "FEAR Whisperer" is the voice of doubt that once spoke negativity into my life. It would speak to me whenever I was unsure how to handle a personal matter. It would cast a shadow of projected failure over an important event or major project that I was tasked to complete. No matter how prepared I was, a voice from nowhere would tell me things like: "Stacy, they are not going to give you that promotion because you are not smart enough." "Your voice will never be heard because you do not speak loud enough." "You cannot reach your destiny because your arms are not long enough." "You do not stand as their equal because you are not tall enough." "You are not loved the way you need to be because you simply do not love yourself enough."

One day I spoke back and told this voice of doubt: "Your

words do not define my destiny, and I have simply had enough!" I had to take a stand against the FEAR-invoking whispers that always lingered near, infusing insecurity and impossibility into my spirit. By repositioning, refocusing and re-establishing myself in God's Word, I found that "His Grace is sufficient for me …" (2 Corinthians 12:9) and that is so much more than enough!

When I think about the meaning of FEAR and how it applies to my life, I reflect on how much time I wasted Finding Excuses And Reasons!

"Finding" is the act of looking for something or someone. Whether it is intentional or unintentional, I kept getting in my own way. God tells me in his Word, "For I know the plans I have for you," declares the Lord, "plans to prosper you and not to harm you, plans to give you hope and a future." (Jeremiah 29:11 NIV)

For whatever reason, I was always curious to know…What does his plan entail? How is he going to carry out his plan? And what am I supposed to do while he works his plan? When I did not get the answers to my questions right away, or things did not turn out the way I thought they should, I felt the need to manipulate the manifestation. In other words, I searched for ways to make my thoughts and notions influence God's plan. By doing so, I was moving according to my perspective rather than walking in his purpose.

"Excuses" are my own personal justifications for not taking action, oftentimes delaying my destiny. Procrastination on my part was fueled by my own desire to know specifics and details of God's plans for me. Rather than just trust him and not doubt, I drew conclusions that were self-defeating. This ultimately cast a shadow of fear over my faith. Over time, I grew in grace and truly learned to live. I leaned on this scripture: Proverbs 3:5-6

NKJV: "Trust in the Lord with all your heart; and, lean not to your own understanding; in all your ways acknowledge him, and he shall direct your paths."

"And" is a conjunction that simply combines words or actions together. Of course, when moving in fear, I often took an incorrect stance, which led to indecisive behavior. For example: I would worry and wonder, pace and pout or cry and complain… when all I needed to do was recall Psalm 46:10, reminds me to "Be still and know that I am God; I will be exalted among the nations. I will be exalted among the earth." This passage of scripture is my assurance that in any situation or circumstance, all I have to do is "Be still and know."

"Reasons" are justification for my thoughts, words or actions. When I took a stance, I did so based on the notion that I had a good reason for doing what I did. It was my decision to make, or the old standard…Because I said so. Honestly, when I find myself conflicted about my reasons, I refer to Proverbs 3:5-6 NKJV. In the realm of purpose, it is imperative that I understand that God's reasons are the ones that truly matter. He is the author and finisher of my faith, as Hebrews 12:2 tells us: Let us fix our eyes on Jesus, the author and perfecter of our faith,

Finding Excuses And Reasons was my FEAR Factor. These days, when I sit down at my dining table, if fear is being served, I simply close my eyes, bow my head and say my grace - just as I do before every meal. After my amen, I open my eyes, look to the heavens, pick up my knife and fork, and when I hear the voice of doubt whisper negative thoughts to me, I say at the top of lungs, "Bon Appetit!"

Then … I eat FEAR for Breakfast!

Let's Pray

Father God in heaven,

Thank you for your unconditional love, amazing grace and unwavering mercy. We seek your guidance in all that we do, and we dedicate ourselves to walk with purpose as we carry out your perfect will for us. May our thoughts, words and actions be pleasing to you as we help others find you along life's journey

n the name of Jesus,

Amen

Journal

What is God speaking to you?

About Dr. Stacy

Dr. Stacy L. Henderson, a native of Savannah, Ga., is a retired Naval officer with over 25 years of military service and experience. She teaches the future generation of leaders as the Senior Naval Science Instructor (SNSI) at Bloom Township High School in Chicago Heights, Ill. She is the first African-American and woman in that position. The Navy JROTC unit has consistently been ranked as a National Distinguished Unit with Honors under her leadership. She is a STEM facilitator for NJROTC Cadet Girls; a partnership with the Women Veterans Rock! (Philadelphia, Pa.) STEM Civic Leadership Institute for JROTC Cadet Girls.

In June 2023, she formed "The Bloom 'Pedal' Pushers," an eSports iRacing team composed of black and girls raising awareness about NJROTC, STEM and representing girls through programs supporting diversity, equity and inclusion. They are currently the reigning eSports iRacing national champions.

Dr. Stacy is a Christian educator, inspirational speaker, businesswoman and an international best-selling. She speaks four languages and has publications in more than 40 language translations, two of which are in the White House Library. Her Stacy's Stocking Stuffers Christmas Charity has provided toys, meals, coats, clothing and monetary support for families around the world since 1991. And, her Spirit of Excellence Youth Leadership Scholarship Program (Stellar Productions) has provided financial assistance for college students since 2009.

She has countless military and civilian accolades, including five Guinness World Records and a 'Key to the City' from eight U.S. locales. She was named Outstanding Georgia Citizen and won a Presidential Lifetime Achievement Award, presented by President Joseph R. Biden, Jr. She is a devoted wife, loving mother and cherished "GiGi."

Dr. Stacy L. Henderson eats FEAR for Breakfast!

Dr. Stacy may be reached at drstacylhenderson@gmail.com.

Today's Scripture

*For God was in Christ, reconciling the world
to himself, no longer counting people's sins
against them. And he gave us this
wonderful message of reconciliation.*

2 Corinthians 5:19

EAT FEAR FOR BREAKFAST

Day 29

COURAGE IN HIM

By Kimmie Renee

God is in your story. He is in the details, my friend! Jesus gave us this message to share with others: No matter what your past looks like; no matter how broken you feel, he has destroyed the sin barrier.

It will no longer be counted against you, and you are no longer separated from our Father. Come, all of you who are weary and burdened; God knows you're hurting. Listen to his urging. This was written on the back of my mom's memorial card in June 2024. It was also my expounded Bible verse in college. My mom did not know this when she chose this as the theme scripture for a Christian women's retreat, nor did she know that she would lead just one year before she would be called home to heaven. God was in those details.

As a hospice chaplain, I can tell you that fear of dying is a real concern if you don't have the peace of God in your life. As a daughter who lost her mom, I can tell you fear will try to invade any space you allow it to enter. My mom was the strongest woman I have ever known, and she taught me that my courage must come from God. If our courage comes from another person and that person is no longer in our lives, we will be left with nothing. If your courage comes from God and you trust in him, you will have the strength to go on, even when everything seems to be falling apart around you. God's promise is that he will give you courage when you are afraid (Job11:18), and knowing God is with us gives us courage to go on through the hardest moments.

Let's Pray

Father God,

Thank you for the promises in your Word that fear is not our portion. Thank you for being with us through every tough time or frustrating time or sad time that we've cried. You are a faithful and loyal God; you never leave us, and you love us so much, you were willing to come here and experience everything we are crying about. You know us and our situations intimately, and when we think we can't go on and everything is impossible, that's when you show up mightily. You begin at impossible, and you never fail to meet us there. Thank you, Jesus, for being our personal savior.

We love you, and we need you, and it's in your mighty name we pray and believe,

Amen

EAT FEAR FOR BREAKFAST

Journal

What is God speaking to you?

About Kimmie

Kimmie Renee is an executive leader with a background in healthcare management, life coaching and chaplaincy. She is also an Amazon best-selling author and the founder and senior mentor of Sisterhood International Inc., a women's ministry that focuses on discipling women in God's extravagant grace through his Word.

When she's not working, you can find her busy volunteering her time as a military chaplain for the

Department of Defense's Georgia State Guard, where she is currently serving as the first female deputy command chaplain in Georgia's history.

Connect with Kimmie:
Email: kimmie@4walkwayz.com
Cell:770-568-6298

EAT FEAR FOR BREAKFAST

Today's Scripture

Peace I leave with you; my peace I give to you; not as the world gives do I give to you. Let not your heart be troubled, neither let it be afraid.

John 14:27

Day 30

LETTING GOD HAVE CONTROL

By Monica Lloyd

Living life has its challenges. There are days when you are up and days when you are down. You might feel as though your emotions are all over the place, not knowing how you might react in the next moment. When this happens, your heart can beat fast, causing you to lose the rhythm of your breathing, and if you are not careful, you will find yourself blacking out. Some will call this anxiety; I call it no peace.

Peace is lost when our intellect is unable to locate answers for our circumstances. When we cannot figure a way out, we become anxious. We enter a realm of bad decision making and make poor choices, one right after the other. I know these feelings, for at one time, they described me.

I was a lady who thought she had life all figured out, but I had no peace. I trusted my abilities more than I trusted God. I would find myself saying, "I got this, God. You can rest today." How foolish was I to tell the creator that he can have a rest day from life? While I might not have spoken those exact words, my actions spoke volumes.

I could not figure out why I tossed and turned throughout the night. My brain was overloaded, running a thousand miles an hour. I repeated aloud: "Lord, help me figure this out," not realizing that it was already figured out, and all that was required of me was to not let my heart be troubled nor let it be afraid. I feared letting God take control; this robbed me of my peace.

Peace is free; it comes as lagniappe when you trust God. The world, however, will keep you on the edge in hopes that one day you fall off. That's why God says in Philippians 4:7 that the peace he gives will guard your heart and mind, meaning it will keep you safe from harm and danger, and it will allow you to sleep at night. His peace is not from the world nor does it operate like the world. You can keep it with you always.

So, go ahead and let go of everything that you believe you have under control, because in reality, this belief is holding you back from receiving your peace.

Let's Pray

Father God,

I surrender my will and way of thinking. I take on the mind of Christ Jesus and humble myself. You are the author of peace, and I accept your peace, for it guides me and keeps me from harm and danger. Thank you for being mindful of me.

In Jesus' name,

Amen

Journal

What is God speaking to you?

About Monica

Monica Lloyd is a woman with an apostolic teaching anointing who can discern the intents of the heart of mankind and bring deliverance through her teachings with the clarity of God's Word. Feeding souls is her mission, helping to bring about complete wholeness through Jesus Christ.

She currently serves as the executive pastor of Unveiled Ministries of Chicago, Ill., under the senior leadership of Apostle Sharon R. Peters-Ruff.

Monica has been in ministry for over 20 years, and her coming into the knowledge of the Lord Jesus Christ has brought her great fulfillment in life as she walks out his plans. She knows that desires without Christ are only self-willed ambitions.

Being in union with her husband, George Lloyd, for 37 years and being a mother of three sons and grandmother to eight children, she has been shown that her that marriage can yet be blissful and fulfilling. She sincerely believes that when God is made the anchor, there will be no uprooting!

Monica has been in ministry for over 20 years, and her coming into the knowledge of the Lord Jesus Christ has brought her great fulfillment in life as she walks out his plans. She knows that desires without Christ are only self-willed ambitions.

Being in union with her husband, George Lloyd, for 37 years and being a mother of three sons and grandmother to eight children, she has been shown that her that marriage can yet be blissful and fulfilling. She sincerely believes that when God is made the anchor, there will be no uprooting!

How to contact Monica:

Facebook - Dr. Monica Lloyd

EAT FEAR FOR BREAKFAST

Made in the USA
Columbia, SC
31 August 2024